OCTOPUSES ONE TO TEN

Written by Ellen Jackson • Illustrated by Robin Page

Beach Lane Books

New York   London   Toronto   Sydney   New Delhi

Octopuses like to hide.
One is safe and snug inside.

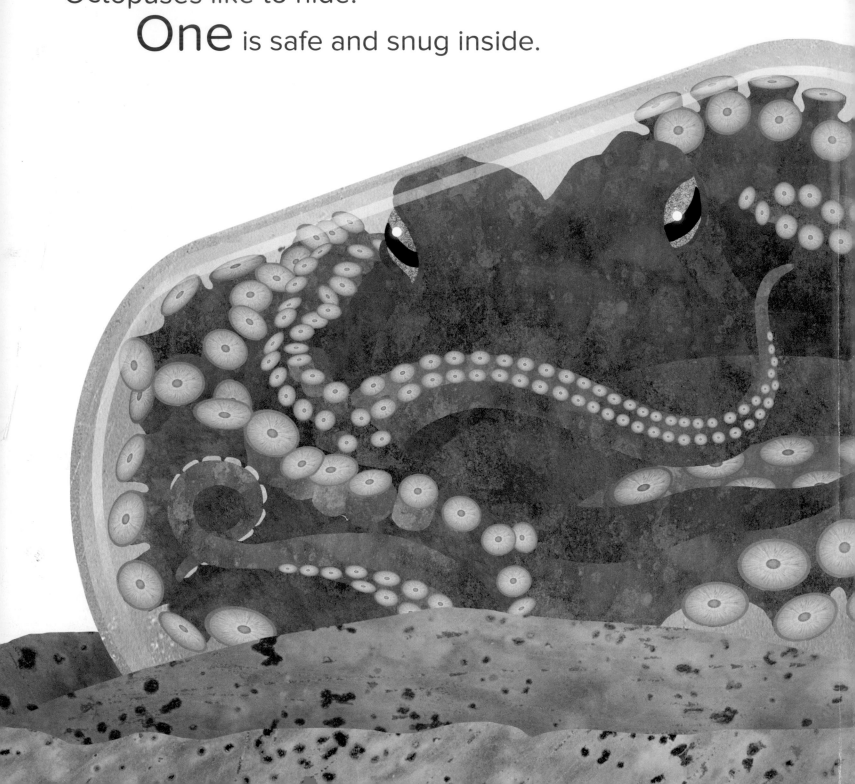

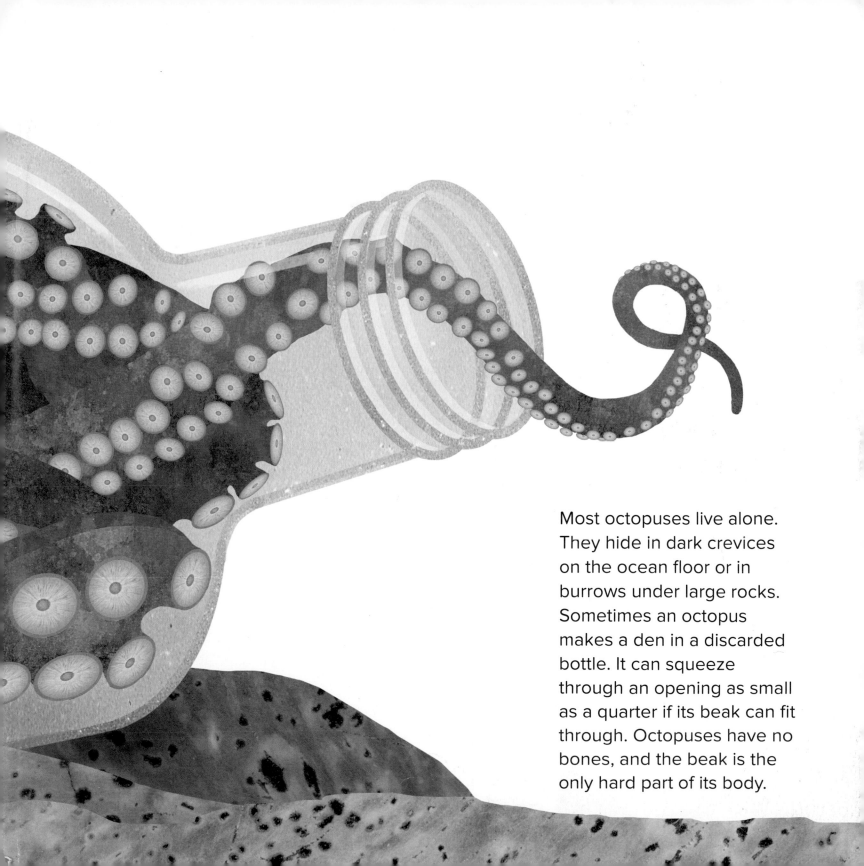

Most octopuses live alone. They hide in dark crevices on the ocean floor or in burrows under large rocks. Sometimes an octopus makes a den in a discarded bottle. It can squeeze through an opening as small as a quarter if its beak can fit through. Octopuses have no bones, and the beak is the only hard part of its body.

Octopuses on patrol
use **two** "legs" to take a stroll.

Octopuses have eight arms. Marine scientists have observed that two of these arms act more like legs. Octopuses sometimes walk across the ocean floor on these two "legs" or push off with them when swimming. In aquariums, octopuses have been known to climb out of their tanks, walk to another fish tank, and dine on the occupants.

Here's an octo-oddity:
   Count each heart—there's one, two, **three!**

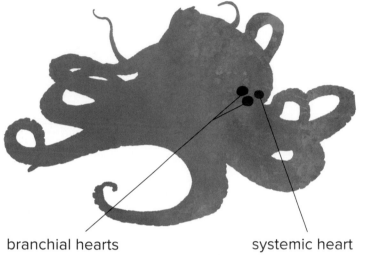

branchial hearts   systemic heart

Octopuses are amazing!
They have three hearts,
bluish-green blood, and the
ability to regrow an arm if
they lose one. Their tongues
are covered with tiny teeth,
which they use to scrape a
small animal from its shell.
The suckers in their arms can
grab objects, cling to rocks,
and even taste prey.

Octopuses in disguise have **four** ways to fool your eyes.

Seals, sharks, dolphins, and whales love to dine on octopus. But octopuses are clever shape-shifters. And they have other ways to stay safe:

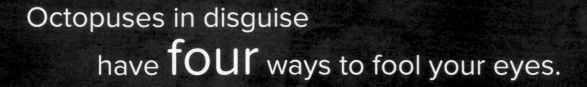

❶ When threatened, they squirt a cloud of black ink. This confuses the predator while the octopus jets away in the opposite direction.

2 If discovered by a predator, they can change their colors and skin texture to blend in with a rock. Some can even make themselves look like a crab, a seashell, or a flatfish.

3 An octopus can detach one of its arms. The arm wriggles off, sending the predator chasing after it.

4 The octopus can simply disappear into its den until the danger passes.

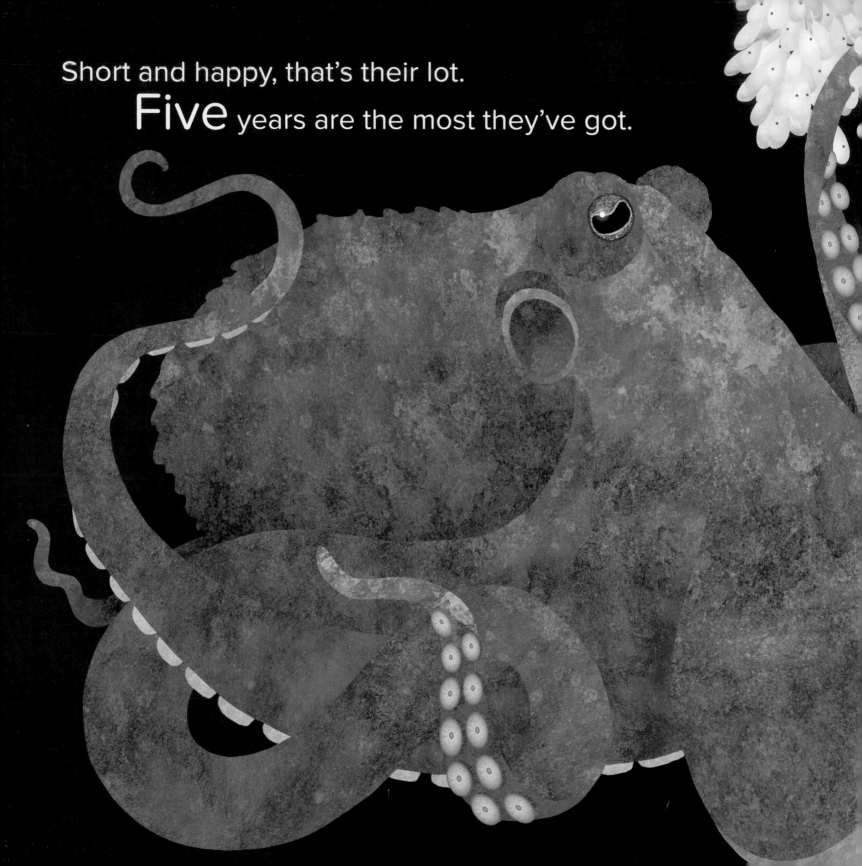

Short and happy, that's their lot.
Five years are the most they've got.

The giant Pacific octopus lives for five years, but some species live for only six months. Females survive long enough to tend their eggs, cleaning and squirting water over them. Each female releases 100,000 to 500,000 eggs, but few of the hatchlings will make it to adulthood.

Six strong arms can help them grab shrimp and lobster, fish and crab.

Octopuses catch prey with six of their eight arms. First they bite the prey with their beak and inject it with a poison. Then they suck or scrape out the meat. Octopuses hunt mostly at night.

They can wander where they please,
swimming through the seven seas.

Every ocean of the world, from the shallow
coastal waters to the depths of the sea, is
home to at least one species of octopus.
They live in the tropics and in the frigid
waters of the Arctic and Antarctic. They live
in coral reefs and on the sandy ocean floor.
The "seven seas" include the Arctic Ocean,
the north Atlantic Ocean, the south Atlantic
Ocean, the Indian Ocean, the north Pacific
Ocean, the south Pacific Ocean, and the
Antarctic Ocean.

Celebrate and give a cheer
on October **eight** each year.

Since octopuses have eight arms (the prefix "octo-" means "eight"), October 8 is their special day. The *Octopus News Magazine Online* forum first established October 8 as a day to recognize this amazing animal. World Octopus Day is now celebrated by the National Aquarium in Baltimore, the Bristol Aquarium, *Scientific American* magazine, and many other aquariums and organizations.

Octopuses! They're so fine.
You have one brain—they have nine!

No wonder octopuses seem so smart! Each octopus arm has a brain of its own, plus one main brain that gives commands to the others. That's right—nine brains! Octopuses can open a jar to get at a crab inside. They even use tools. Common octopuses will collect small objects and pile them outside their dens to hide the entrance. Veined octopuses carry coconut shell halves to use as a shelter if they're attacked.

Here are **ten** that you might meet—
all with arms and none with feet!

❶ The giant Pacific octopus is portrayed throughout this book. This octopus, one of the largest, can recognize individual humans.

❷ This octopus has been found in the Atlantic Ocean and off the coast of New Zealand. Males appear to have seven arms because one is hidden in a sack below their right eye.

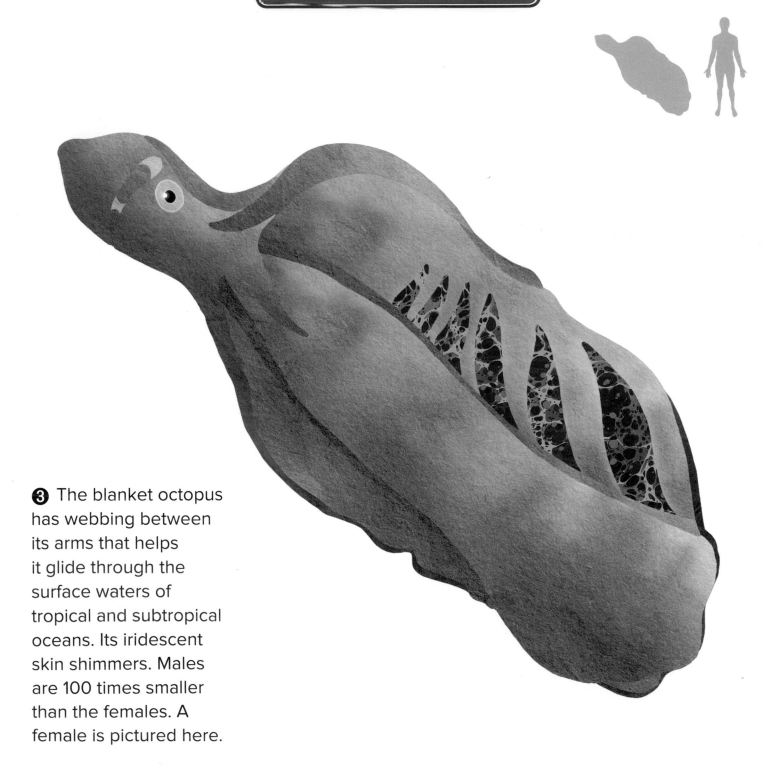

❸ The blanket octopus has webbing between its arms that helps it glide through the surface waters of tropical and subtropical oceans. Its iridescent skin shimmers. Males are 100 times smaller than the females. A female is pictured here.

❹ Like many other species, the common octopus can mimic the colors, textures, and patterns of the objects around it. It's found in both tropical and temperate waters of the Atlantic Ocean.

❺ The mimic octopus can take on the shape and behavior of more than fifteen different sea animals, including a jellyfish, a lionfish, and a stingray. The mimic octopus lives off the coasts of Indonesia and Malaysia.

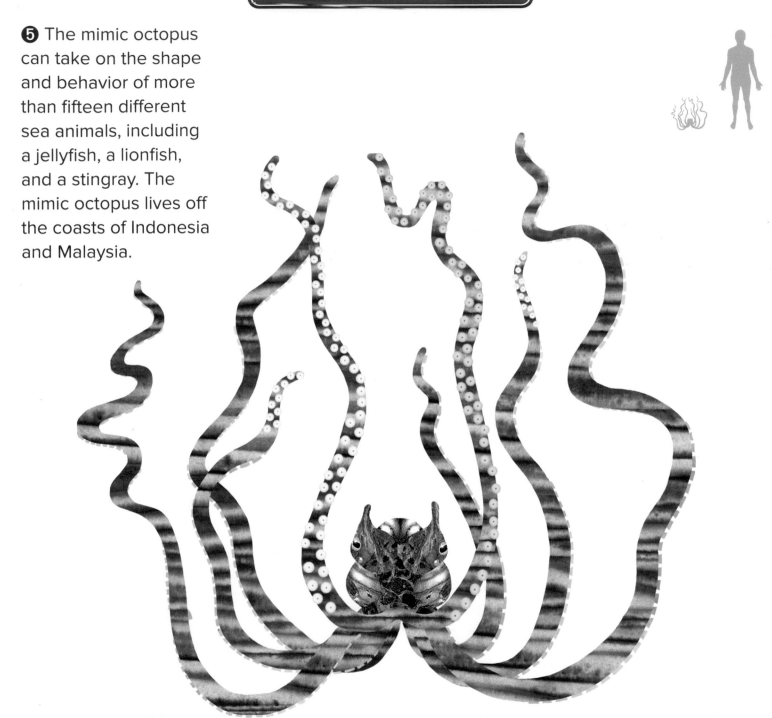

❻ The Dumbo octopus has one paddle-shaped fin on each side of its headlike body. These fins resemble the ears of Dumbo, an animated character in a Walt Disney movie. Dumbo octopuses usually live at a depth of 3,000 to 4,000 meters (9,800 to 13,000 feet).

7 The blue-ringed octopus of Australia is known as one of the most poisonous marine animals. Its venom can kill a human.

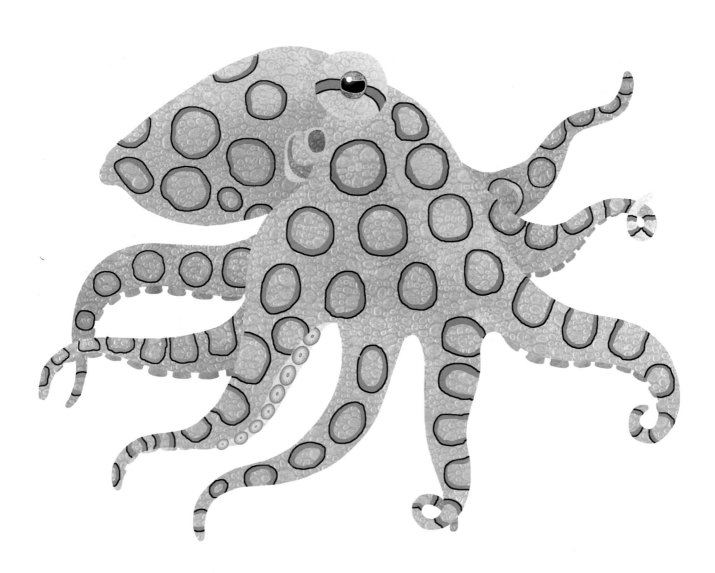

8 Larger Pacific striped octopuses mate face-to-face and press their beaks and suckers against each other. Found along the Pacific coasts of Panama and Nicaragua, they live in groups of up to 40.

❾ The veined octopus is found in the tropical waters of the western Pacific Ocean. It gathers and uses coconuts and shells for shelter.

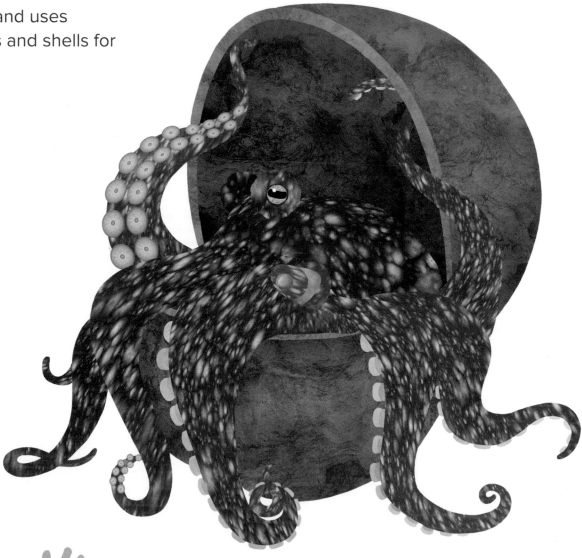

❿ The wolfi is one of the smallest octopuses in the world. Found in the Indo-Pacific Ocean, a full-grown wolfi is only 1.5 centimeters (a half inch) in length.

Octopuses near and far,
each an eight-armed superstar!

Banana Octopus

Remove a banana from its peel. Fringe the bottom of the peel with scissors to make the eight arms and stuff the top with tissue paper to make the head. Add googly eyes with glue.

Toilet Paper Roll Octopus

You will need:
Glue
Scissors
Toilet paper
Cardboard toilet paper
    tube
Paintbrush
White primer paint
Green or blue paint
Googly eyes
Black pen

1. Roll the toilet paper into a ball that will fit halfway into the top of the tube. Glue it in place. Half of the paper ball should stick out to form the head.
2. Brush white primer paint all over the toilet paper tube and head with a brush. Let the paint dry.

3. Paint the tube and head with the blue or green paint.
4. Cut straight lines one third of the way up from the bottom of the tube for the arms. You can paint the bottom of the arms too.
5. Glue on the googly eyes and draw the mouth with the pen.

Oreo Octopuses

Use oreo cookies for the head and body and gummy worms for the arms.

Healthy Octopus Candy

You will need:
honey
powdered milk
peanut butter
raisins

Make modeling dough by combining equal parts honey, powdered milk, and peanut butter. If it's too sticky, add more powdered milk. Mold it into the shape of an octopus and add raisins for eyes. Enjoy!

RESOURCES FOR FURTHER LEARNING AND EXPLORATION

Langeland, Deirdre. *Octopus' Den*. Norwalk, CT: Soundprints, 1997.

Lindeen, Carol K. *Octopuses*. North Mankato, MN: Capstone Press, 2005.

Montgomery, Sy. *The Octopus Scientists: Exploring the Mind of a Mollusk*. Boston: Houghton Mifflin Harcourt, 2015.

Montgomery, Sy. *The Soul of an Octopus: A Surprising Exploration into the Wonder of Consciousness*. New York: Atria Books, 2015.

Srinivasan, Divya. *Octopus Alone*. New York: Viking, 2013.

PBS Kids

Giant Pacific octopus video: http://pbskids.org/video/?guid=00b6423c-da19-4d91-9008-a9195001c1dc

Monterey Bay Aquarium

Facts about the red octopus: http://www.montereybayaquarium.org/animals-and-experiences/exhibits/giant-octopus

Vancouver Aquarium

Octopuses and squids: https://www.vanaqua.org/learn/aquafacts/invertebrates/octopuses-and-squids

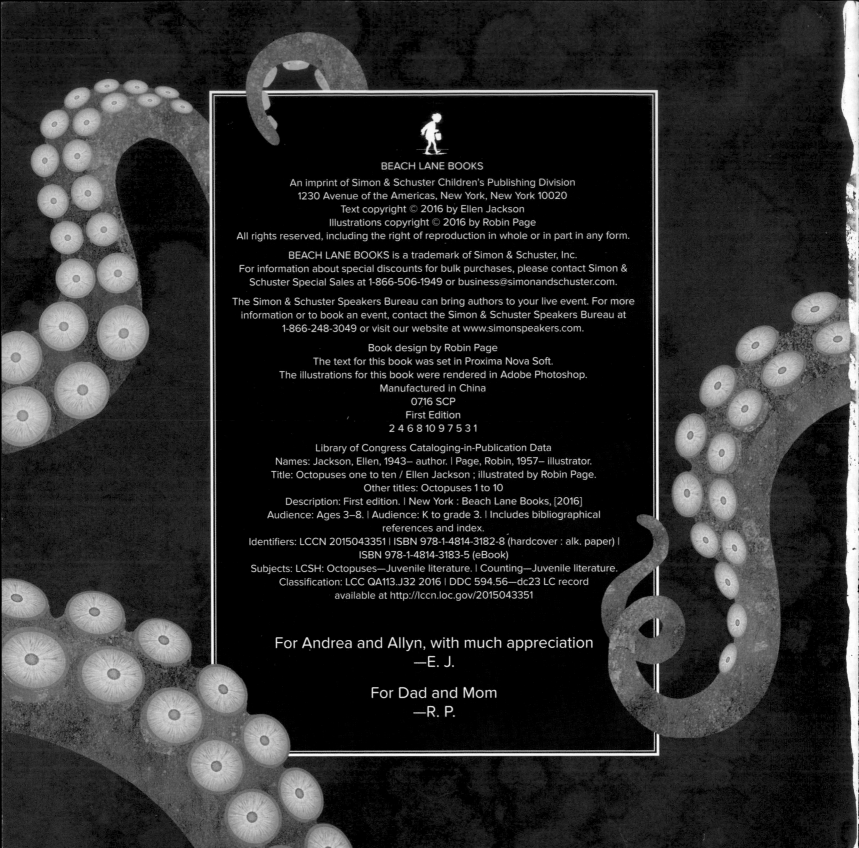

BEACH LANE BOOKS

An imprint of Simon & Schuster Children's Publishing Division
1230 Avenue of the Americas, New York, New York 10020
Text copyright © 2016 by Ellen Jackson
Illustrations copyright © 2016 by Robin Page

BEACH LANE BOOKS is a trademark of Simon & Schuster, Inc.
For information about special discounts for bulk purchases, please contact Simon &
Schuster Special Sales at 1-866-506-1949 or business@simonandschuster.com.

The Simon & Schuster Speakers Bureau can bring authors to your live event. For more
information or to book an event, contact the Simon & Schuster Speakers Bureau at
1-866-248-3049 or visit our website at www.simonspeakers.com.

Book design by Robin Page
The text for this book was set in Proxima Nova Soft.
The illustrations for this book were rendered in Adobe Photoshop.
Manufactured in China
0716 SCP
First Edition
2 4 6 8 10 9 7 5 3 1

Library of Congress Cataloging-in-Publication Data
Names: Jackson, Ellen, 1943– author. | Page, Robin, 1957– illustrator.
Title: Octopuses one to ten / Ellen Jackson ; illustrated by Robin Page.
Other titles: Octopuses 1 to 10
Description: First edition. | New York : Beach Lane Books, [2016]
Audience: Ages 3–8. | Audience: K to grade 3. | Includes bibliographical
references and index.
Identifiers: LCCN 2015043351 | ISBN 978-1-4814-3182-8 (hardcover : alk. paper) |
ISBN 978-1-4814-3183-5 (eBook)
Subjects: LCSH: Octopuses—Juvenile literature. | Counting—Juvenile literature.
Classification: LCC QA113.J32 2016 | DDC 594.56—dc23 LC record
available at http://lccn.loc.gov/2015043351

For Andrea and Allyn, with much appreciation
—E. J.

For Dad and Mom
—R. P.